Madonna

Madonna

Julia Holt

Published in association with The Basic Skills Agency

Hodder & Stoughton

A MEMBER OF THE HODDER HEADLINE GROUP

Acknowledgements

*Photos: pp. 8, 13, 31 © Corbis, pp. 17, 21 © Alpha,
p. 28 © Redferns, p. 35 © Popperfoto,
p. 37 © Jean Cummings/All Action.*

Cover photo: © O'Brian/Peters/All Action.

Orders: please contact Bookpoint Ltd, 39 Milton Park, Abingdon, Oxon OX14 4TD. Telephone: (44) 01235 400414, Fax: (44) 01235 400454. Lines are open from 9.00–6.00, Monday to Saturday, with a 24 hour message answering service. Email address: orders@bookpoint.co.uk

British Library Cataloguing in Publication Data
A catalogue record for this title is available from The British Library

ISBN 0 340 71150 7

First published 1998
Impression number 10 9 8 7 6 5 4 3
Year 2002 2001 2000 1999

Typeset by Fakenham Photosetting Ltd, Fakenham, Norfolk.
Printed in Great Britain for Hodder & Stoughton Educational, a division of Hodder Headline Plc, 338 Euston Road, London NW1 3BH by Redwood Books, Trowbridge, Wiltshire.

Contents

Madonna is one of the most successful women
in the history of pop music.
Her talent and her ambition
have taken her to the very top.

Nothing in her early life
showed what was to come.
Madonna's Grandparents
came to the USA from Italy.
They were looking for a better life.

Their sixth son Tony moved to Detroit
to work in the car industry.
He married a lovely French-Canadian woman
called Madonna Louise.
They lived in a small brick bungalow
near Detroit.

They had six children:
Little Tony, Martin, Madonna,
Paula, Christopher and Melanie.

1 Childhood

Madonna Louise was born at her
Grandmother's house
in Bay City on 16 August 1958.
Everyone called her 'Little Nonni'.
Madonna's parents were never strict
when their six children were in trouble.
But they were strict about going to church.
Every morning at 6am, come rain or shine,
the family went to church for an hour.
Then the children got the bus
to the Catholic school
and their parents went to work.

One year after Melanie was born,
Madonna's mother died of breast cancer.
Madonna was five years old.
The little girl was scared that her Dad
might die as well.
So she kept close to him
and tried very hard to please him.
For two years she only left his side
to go to school.

Tony always gave his children 50 cents
when they got an A at school.
Madonna made sure she always got As.

She was a very pretty child and she knew it.
Her brothers and sisters often ganged up on her.
Once when they were playing outside
they hung her up by her pants
on the washing line.
Madonna felt like an outsider in her own home.

Tony married his housekeeper
three years after his wife's death.
Her name was Joan.
Tony told his children to call her 'Mom'
and they didn't like it.
They wanted their real Mom back.
Madonna felt like her Dad had left her.
She told herself 'I don't need anybody'.
Then she lived her life trying to prove it.

The family moved to a bigger house.
Madonna had to look after
the three youngest children
and her new half brother and sister.
She had to babysit and wash and clean.
She could not wait to get away.

All the children had music lessons
but Madonna hated hers.
She asked for dance lessons instead
and she loved them.

Madonna tried hard to be different at school.
She wore coloured socks and pants.
Anything to be different from the other kids.

At a school talent show
the other kids sang or played music.
She painted herself green
and danced in a bikini.
This shocked her Dad.
He grounded her for a week.
But everyone else clapped loudly.

Madonna was always in trouble at school.
She was always talking too much or chasing boys.
She wanted to have fun
like the boys had.
But she still got As on her report card.

In her teens she started to rebel.
She shoplifted with her friends.
She drove round in her red Mustang
instead of going to church.
Once Madonna and her friend did go to church
but they only wore coats and nothing else.
They sat at the back giggling.

When Madonna left school
her dance teacher told her to apply
for a place to study dance at college.
She got the place
but again she was an outsider.
She didn't fit in.

The other students looked like ballet dancers.
Madonna had black, punk style hair
and a torn dance outfit,
held together with safety pins.

So in 1978 she dropped out.

2 New York

At the age of 19, Madonna left home
and went to New York.
Madonna tried to make it as a dancer.
She did get to dance
but she didn't make much money.
At times she looked in dustbins for food.
She looked for burgers,
but she threw away the meat
because she was a vegetarian.

To earn more money she
did lots of different jobs.
She worked in shops.
She was a nude model.
She starred in a cheap horror film.

During this time
Madonna became interested in making music.
She learned to play the guitar and the drums.
She also started to write songs
and she got work in Paris as a backing singer.
But she was soon back in New York
and she made up her mind to be a star.

Madonna joined a band called
'The Breakfast Club'.
She was their drummer and singer.
She was learning fast.
In 1980 she started her own band called 'Emmy',
which was one of her nicknames.
They played all the worst clubs in New York.

Madonna still didn't have much money.
She slept on friends' floors
until they asked her to go.
She rode a bike everywhere.
She ate a lot of popcorn to fill herself up.

Her short hair was a different colour every week.
No-one else looked like her.
She learned to be pushy to get what she wanted.

In 1981 she signed with Gotham Productions.
Now she had a manager.
They gave her a place to live
and some pocket money.

But she still had to work as a cleaner
to make money for food.
So she cleaned by day
and wrote songs by night.
She sent her demo tape to
all the record companies.

After two years' hard work
she still didn't have a recording contract.
So Madonna left Gotham Productions.

She went back to squat in an office block
and eat popcorn.
At night she took her new demo tape
round all the clubs.
She got the tape played and got herself known.

3 The Big Break

In 1982 a star DJ called Mark Kamins
gave Madonna her big break.
He took her demo tape
to Warner Brothers' Sire Records.
They liked the tape and they liked Madonna
with her new blonde hairstyle.

She signed with them.
For the first time,
Madonna didn't have to beg
or look in bins for food.

Her first album came out in 1983.
It was called 'Madonna'.
She made it a success in the clubs
by going and dancing along to her own songs.

One track called 'Holiday'
was soon being played on the radio.
Then it went in to America's Top 20.
'Lucky Star' and 'Borderline' came out as singles
and they were hits too.

As soon as the album was a hit,
Sire records let Madonna
make videos for the singles.
The videos were shown on MTV.
This was the first time that the world saw
the Madonna look.
She wore short skirts, with a bare midriff,
a torn t-shirt, lace gloves and crucifixes.

Many of Madonna's critics said
she was a one-hit wonder.
But the next two years proved them wrong.

She got herself a new manager.
His name was Freddy de Mann.
He was Michael Jackson's manager.

In November 1983 she had a small part
in the film 'Vision Quest'.
A song from that film gave her
a No 1 hit in the USA.
It was called 'Crazy For You'.

In the summer of 1984
she finished her second album, 'Like A Virgin'.
Then she went to Venice to make a video for it.
She danced in a gondola wearing
a white wedding dress.
'Like A Virgin' sold 11 million copies.

Back in New York,
they were looking for someone
to play a punk rocker
in the film 'Desperately Seeking Susan'.
Madonna wanted the part and she got it.
She was paid $8,000 for it.
The star was paid five times more.

When the film came out, Madonna was the star.
She even had a UK No 1 hit from the film.
It was called 'Into The Groove'.
The film and her second album
were hits at the same time.
Stardom had arrived for Madonna.

She went on to have three more hits
from her second album.
One of them was 'Material Girl'.
In the video for the single
she dressed as Marilyn Monroe.

Some said Madonna *was* the material girl.
She always made sure
that she was in control of her own career.

4 Marriage

In 1985
she sold more albums and singles than anyone else
and she met Sean Penn.

They met when she was making the video
for 'Material Girl'.
He came from a rich family.
He was one of Hollywood's bad boys
both on and off the screen.

Madonna was seen as the bad girl
of the music industry.
She had many lovers before Sean.
When she met him
she was also seeing the singer Prince.

They both came to see her
on her first tour of the USA.
The Virgin Tour was a big success.
Tickets sold out in record time.
Many of her women fans were dressed like her.
The shops were full of lace and crucifixes.

Madonna on tour

In July 1985 Madonna sang at the Live Aid concert.
She was introduced as:
'a woman who pulled herself up by her bra straps
and who has been known to let them down'.
Nude photos of Madonna, taken years ago,
were now in Playboy.

Madonna's friends were worried
when she said she was marrying Sean.
He had a bad temper
and was often in trouble with the police.
He didn't like gay people
and a lot of her friends were gay.
But she was happy
and like any other 26 year old
she made a lot of plans for her wedding.

They were married on her birthday
at a friend's house in Malibu.
No press were allowed,
and none of the guests were told where to go
until the day before.

Some of the press flew over in a helicopter.
Sean went out and fired a gun at them.

At 6.30pm they were married
in front of 220 guests.
Sean wore a cheap suit
and Madonna wore a white dress and a black hat.
From then on
they were known as the 'Poison Penns'.

Soon after the wedding,
Sean's drinking started to worry Madonna.
She went to a therapist for help.
He just got into more fights.
He even went to prison for a short time.

They made a film together.
It was called 'Shanghai Surprise'.
It was a big flop.
Madonna reacted to the flop
by changing her image.
Out went the brashy, trashy look.
Out went the lace and the crucifixes.
In came a fresher look,
but she kept the red lips and the beauty spot.

Madonna's next album was called 'True Blue'.
It came out in 1986 and sold 17 million copies.
With this album Madonna showed her critics
that she could write good songs.

Five top ten singles came from the album.
'Live To Tell' was the first hit
and Sean used it in one of his films.

Next came 'Papa Don't Preach'.
This song is about a teenager
telling her father that she is having a baby.

Madonna wanted to make another film with Sean.
But when 'Shanghai Surprise' came out
she changed her mind.
Now she wanted to work on her own.
She wanted the star part in the film 'Evita',
but the film was held up.
It was to be ten years before she got her wish.

Madonna in the film 'Who's That Girl?'

5 Who's That Girl?

The film she did make in 1986
was called 'Who's That Girl'.
It was another flop.
But the Who's That Girl World Tour was not.
Madonna went into training for the tour
and she lost ten pounds.
She wore eight outfits for the shows
and each one showed a different side of her.
Some were sexy, some serious and some funny.
Madonna looked every inch a star.

But her marriage was not going as well.
Sean and Madonna were always splitting up
and getting back together again.
He went everywhere with a loaded gun.
He shot at photos of her friends.

At an AIDS benefit in 1987
the stress showed in her face.
They had a fight before the benefit
and it carried on afterwards.
Then Sean stormed out.

In 1988 Sean came home
from filming in the Far East.
He saw press reports that Madonna was bi-sexual.
She had made friends
with a woman called Sandra Bernhardt.
They went everywhere together
and told wild stories on TV chat shows.
Sean and Sandra hated one another.

Madonna was away from the charts
for most of 1989.
She was in a play for eight months.
It was called 'Speed The Plough'.
But she had been writing songs at the same time.
Those songs were for her new album.

It came out late in 1989.
It was called 'Like A Prayer'.
This was the album
that made her critics eat their words.
It gave her five more smash hits.

Pepsi paid her $5 million
to be in one of their adverts.
The advert had her music playing
in the background.
But Pepsi didn't know Madonna's plans
for her 'Like A Prayer' video.
It showed her dancing in front of burning crosses
and kissing a black saint.
Pepsi were shocked.
They dropped the advert
but she kept the money.
Madonna learned that making the headlines
makes money.
'Like A Prayer' was her fastest selling single.

Over Christmas 1989
Sean broke into Madonna's house.
He tied her to a chair and beat her for two hours.
That was the end.
She divorced him in January 1990.

Madonna picked herself up again.
She asked her brother Christopher
to find her a new house.
It was a $3 million house
up in the Hollywood Hills.
She filled the house with beautiful paintings.
She paid for some of them
with the money she got from Pepsi.

Madonna asked Warren Beatty
for a part in his new film, 'Dick Tracy'.
She wanted the part of Breathless Mahoney.
She said she would do it
for less money than anyone else
and so she got it.

In the Spring of 1990,
Madonna made the video for her next single.
It was called 'Express Yourself'
and it went to No 1.
Then in the Summer she played Breathless
in the film Dick Tracy.

Madonna always plans ahead.
So, when she was making the film
she was also planning her next tour.
It was called 'The Blonde Ambition Tour'.

Her advert for dancers said:
'Wimps and wannabees need not apply'.
Madonna wanted the tour to be shocking.

At 31 she was the centre of an industry.
Madonna owned many companies
like Siren Films and Boy Toy inc.
In the past five years she had earned $150 million.
She was the highest paid woman in the industry.

But she wanted to hide her talent for business
from her fans.
In the film of The Blonde Ambition Tour
none of her business meetings were filmed.
She knew what the fans wanted to see.

The film of the tour was called
'In Bed With Madonna'.
It showed her singing on stage
and joking with her dancers back stage.
One of the songs she sang was 'Vogue'.
It was her eighth No 1 hit single
and the biggest selling single of 1990.

Vogue was on the album of songs
from the film Dick Tracy.
In the end Madonna earned $20 million
from that album.
So it didn't matter how much she was paid
to be in the film.

When the tour came to Madonna's home town
her family came to see her.
She cut out some of the sexy parts of her show
because her Dad was there.
She got him onto the stage
and everyone sang 'Happy Birthday' to him.

Sadly, not everyone
in Madonna's family was happy.
Her brother Martin had to go to a clinic to dry out.
Mario was in trouble with the Police over drugs.
Also Paula was said to be jealous of her half sister.

In a TV show Madonna told the world
that Christopher was a gay man
before he had chance to tell his Dad.
Sometimes Madonna went too far.
But to her fans Madonna could do no wrong.

Dick Tracy was a success when it came out.
Chanel said that she set the style
for the fashion world.
She was voted
one of America's most powerful women.
Was there anything left to do?

She didn't need to work anymore
but she still needed to shock.

In 1991 her greatest hits album came out.
It was called 'The Immaculate Collection'.
She made a very sexy video
for a single from the album.
It was called 'Justify My Love'.
When MTV saw it they banned it
and she had another hit on her hands.
Sales from the video came to $2.5 million
and the single went to No 1.

Then 'In Bed With Madonna' came out.
It started out
as Madonna's home video of her tour,
but by the end it was a film.
She went to Cannes to show the film.
She wore a long red cape
with only her bra and pants under it.
The cameras clicked.
The film was a hit.

Madonna wins another award

Madonna signed a multi-million dollar deal
with Time Warner.
The deal allowed her
to run her own record company, Maverick.
Her business life was a success
but her personal life was a mess.
She missed Sean and she wanted a baby.

The fans were waiting for her next album.
It came in 1992.
It was called 'Erotica',
and the title single went right to the top.
Madonna had three more hits from the album.
But by then everyone's eyes were on her book.

It was called 'Sex'.
The book came wrapped in tin foil
so that no-one saw it
until they had paid for it.
It sold out everywhere.

In the long run the last album and the book
were a mistake.
She had gone too far.
People had seen too much of her
and they switched off.

In the next three years she had small parts
in five more films.
Most of them were flops.

She also made two more albums.
The first was 'Bedtime Stories' in 1994.
Her fans did not like it much.
But she did have a No 1 single from it
called 'Take A Bow'.

In 1995
her album called 'Something To Remember'
showed that she could sing slow songs.
One single from that album was a hit.
It was called 'You'll See'.

6 Evita

What Madonna needed
was another change of style.

The new Madonna was first seen in 1996.
She was in the hit film 'Evita'.
And in the same year she became a mother.

The part of 'Evita'
is one she had waited for ten years to play.
She seemed to be born to play it.
Madonna was given a Golden Globe award
for her acting in the film.

Then in October 1996
Lourdes Maria was born in an LA hospital.
Her father is Carlos Leon.
He was Madonna's fitness trainer.
Madonna has shown no plans
to settle down with him.
But she is very happy to be a mother at last.

Madonna in the film 'Evita'.

Madonna has shown all along
that she has a good head for business.
Her record company Maverick
has just signed The Prodigy and Erasure.

She has shown that she can write songs
not just for herself
but for others, like Gary Barlow.

She also has the star part
in a Mick Jagger film.
It's about the photographer Tina Modotti.

Madonna may not shock us anymore
but she will carry on making money
because she is a very clever business woman.

If you have enjoyed reading this book, you may be interested in other titles in the *Livewire* series.

The following titles are available on famous people from the worlds of film and music:

The Spice Girls
Whitney Houston
Gangsta!
Tina Turner
Arnold Schwarzenegger
Clint Eastwood
Marilyn Monroe
Keanu Reeves
Mel Gibson
John Travolta
Michelle Pfeiffer
Pulp
Oasis
Michael Jackson